The Life of Dave
as Told by Himself

Frank E. Butler

with Additional Material

Published by Plesner Publishing, Riverboat Landing Imprint
Leesburg, Florida

ISBN: 979-8-9997740-4-0 (paperback)
979-8-9997740-5-7 (hardcover)
Printed in the United States of America

Table of Contents

Annie and Frank Butler along with Dave

Annie shooting an apple off of Dave's head

The *Newark Sunday Call*, June 24, 1923

Printed from the "Newark Sunday Call" June 24, 1923, pages 53 and 54

NEWARK SUNDAY CALL

"Dave"--Annie Oakley's Wonder Dog Passes to Happy Hunting Grounds

————

This is the plain story of a dog bearing the plain name Dave, but not a plain dog himself. He was a beautiful setter, owned by Frank E. Butler and his wife, Annie Oakley Butler, and for ten years he was their faithful companion. Wherever they lived, and ofttimes they put up at the finest hotels in the land, Dave was ever a third guest. Everywhere that Annie went the dog was sure to go. In shooting practice or exhibitions Miss Oakley, who was the world's premier woman rifle shot, often would shoot an apple from Dave's head at a range of fifty yards. Standing on his hind haunches in such a test of accuracy, the dog never blinked an eye, knowing that the aim of his gentle mistress, was as unerring as William Tell's when he sent an arrow from his trusty bow piercing an apple of the head of his son.

Now, Dave, the setter, is no more. He was killed recently in an automobile smash-up at Leesburg, Florida, and his soul passed on to the happy hunting grounds. Like Black Beauty, the horse, and Beautiful Joe, the dog, broke into print with stories of their lives, so the career of Dave is now extolled in a booklet entitled "The Life of Dave." It is an autobiography supposed to have been written by Dave himself, the contents suggested by Miss Oakley in a quiet retreat at Merchantville, N. J. If you're interested in a plain story of an exceptional dog read on:

THE LIFE OF DAVE
As Told by Himself.

I have often heard my friends and admirers say, "I wish you could talk, so you could tell us what you are thinking about." I suppose they meant well, but I always got along very nicely without talking, and from my own observations I find that many people get in trouble by talking too much. Anyway, I got along very well, for I could always understand my master and my mistress; I never had any trouble in making them understand me when I wanted anything.

I have been told many times that I was quite a celebrity. My master and mistress have shown me my pictures in papers and I have seen myself in the movies. Many nice ladies said I was a handsome dog, and I guess I was, but I always felt better pleased when they said that I was a good dog—not that I deserve any credit for being good; my master and mistress were always so kind to me that I could not have been otherwise, and now that I am getting on in years and not hunting any more, I find time hangs heavy, so I have decided to write my life and dedicate it to my many friends.

I know many dogs look back to their puppy days as the happiest hours of their lives. I would gladly forget mine if I could do so. My earliest recollection is that I was one of several dogs, some small like myself, which I heard a man say were my brothers and sisters. No one had to tell me who my mother was. Instinct told me that, and while she was a good mother to us all, I could see that she favored me. She certainly was a beautiful dog and won prizes on the bench at many shows. I never saw my father, but heard he was a field trial winner. His name was California Bell Boy and I often heard people say that I looked like him.

We all romped and played together, quarreled and made up again, the same as I have often seen other children do. Our kennel was none too clean and our food none too plentiful, but we were a happy lot and growing bigger every day.

One night a man came in, and after looking us over, took one away in a basket. That happened several times, until only my mother and myself were left. I heard my master say he would never sell me or my mother, so I was happy with her, but lonesome, until one day another dog was put in with us. I heard my master call him "Chick." He was a very nice fellow and we soon became good friends. One day a man put him in a car and took him away, and again I was very lonesome, for I was no longer a little puppy and my mother paid little if any attention to me now.

Adopted By the Butlers.

One day my master came to the shed where my mother and I were penned up. He had another man with him, who examined me very close-ly, patting my head, and said, "He will do." Then I knew I had been sold and had a new master, and also that I was going to like him; and when he said, "Come on, Dave," I followed him to a wagon and jumped in. As it was getting dark and cold, I got down close to him and he covered me up with a blanket. I heard my new master say we had a twelve-miles' drive. As this was my first trip away from my so-called home, I was glad to get away. Little did I think then that I was to have many homes, but one master and mistress only.

When we arrived at our destination my master put me in a stall in a stable with a pointer named Frank. We had plenty of clean straw and room enough for several more dogs. A little later my master came back and brought us our supper. This being my first meal that day, it sure did taste good. I found Frank a very companionable fellow. He said he didn't belong to my master, but wished he did, as he received better treatment than at his own home.

Off For a Hunt.

The next morning my master came in early and told us we were going hunting and had ten miles to drive, so Frank and I got into the wagon. Then I met my new mistress for the first time. She spoke to me so kindly and gently while patting my head and rubbing my ears, that I knew then I would love her and would always do so. When we arrived at the hunt-ing grounds we were turned loose. Frank had several years' training. I had never been hunting and didn't know what was required of me. So naturally I made some mistakes, but my master didn't whip me, but gave me to understand I must do as he wanted and not as I wanted to do.

A little later Frank came to a point, and when a quail got up I was surprised to see my mistress bring it down. I wanted to get that bird and bring it to her, but Frank got it. Instead of bringing it to her, he dropped it down in a muskrat hole, where he left it and went on hunting. I went to the hole and after much routing and digging I got the bird, brought it to my mistress, and when she patted my head and said, "Good boy, Dave," I was a proud dog. We had lunch under a big tree. Frank and I had a biscuit each, so were ready for the afternoon.

When I was not hunting, my mistress spent hours in training me to what I should do. She told me a good dog should be a gentleman in the house as well as in the field. She was so sweet, patient and gentle that I couldn't help loving her, and I tried hard to make her understand that I wanted to please her.

I lived with them in a hotel, had my own rug in a corner of the bathroom, and I made up my mind that the life of a dog with such a master and mistress was not so bad. One day my mistress called my master in and told me she wanted me to do the tricks she had taught me. I jumped, retrieved eggs she had hidden, got up in a chair, bowed my head and many other things which was a surprise to my master, as he didn't know she had been teaching me.

One day when I was hunting with my master I started to cross a road, when an automobile came around a corner, going very fast. I didn't see it until it struck me on the shoulder and threw me in a ditch.

The driver didn't stop. My master saw it all and I could see him run across the field and fire a shot. Then he came and picked me up, saying,` "If I had buck shot I would have stopped him. Anyone who wouldn't stop after doing that to a dog would have kept on going if it had been a child." I felt sore all over and couldn't walk, but my master carried me back to the wagon. He let me lie on his overcoat on the way home, then my mistress bathed my shoulder in hot water, but it was a long time before I could do any more hunting and my shoulder never did get well. I also had one broken rib that never mended.

Some time after my accident the owners of bird dogs got up what they called a field trial, which was a meeting of all the bird dogs. Each one was to show what he could do by finding and handling birds. There were prizes for the three best dogs. I heard my master say I came from field trial stock and if my shoulder wouldn't go back on me I would win. There were twenty-seven dogs entered. I went into the finals, and had my right leg and shoulder held out I could have won the first prize, but I had to be satisfied with the third, which my master said was fine and that I was a game dog, as I ran the race on three legs.

New Home.

My master and mistress had just finished a new home a few miles from town. It was on the banks of a beautiful river, surrounded by fields and trees; so we all moved there and we liked it very much. Here I was taught to be a watch dog at nights and also to keep an eye on the tramps by day. Chick found out where I was and came to see me quite often. He spent the night with me, and we slept in the garage. We had good beds; the window was left open so we could see or hear if any prowlers came around, but I heard a neighbor say my mistress was such a good shot no one would trouble us.

We were all very happy until my mistress was taken ill and went away. My master told me she had gone to a hospital to undergo an operation. I missed her very much. One day my master asked me if I wanted to see my mistress. I jumped, rolled over and barked to let him know I did. So we got into an automobile and went to a big building; then up to a room where my mistress was lying in bed. There was a woman dressed in white sitting beside her. When I saw my mistress I forgot my manners and jumped up on the bed, something I had never done before or since. She didn't scold me, but let me lick her hands and face, then I knew I was for-given. A few days later she came home and once more we were all happy.

One night I saw my master getting his gun and hunting clothes out of the closet. He saw I was interested and told me we were going hunting. Early next morning a man came with the team and hunting wagon and we all got in. Then I saw a pointer that I had never met before. At first he wasn't very sociable, so I paid no attention to him, but lay down close to my master's feet. Later, when we started hunting, he became very friend-ly and I found he was well trained, so we had a nice day's hunting.

Birds were scarce and we covered a lot of ground. Late in the afternoon our masters decided to start home, as we had a long way to go and it was getting very cold. I saw a marsh that looked like a good place to find birds so I went there and soon found myself in a water hole that I didn't see until too late. My master dried me as best he could before putting me in the wagon, covered me up with some straw and a piece of sacking, but I was very cold on the way home. My mistress rubbed me with towels, covering me up, and I went to sleep. But not for long; I could hardly breathe and felt sore all over. I heard my mistress say it was pneumonia, and she worked over me all night.

Sick For Three Days.

I was a very sick dog for three days. I know I would have died if it had not been for my dear mistress. I made up my mind then that the life they had saved would be dedicated to them. We all spent a pleasant winter in the Maryland home. As it was very cold, my mistress moved my bed into the house. Each night we had a big open fire and as I had the run of the house, I also had my share of the fire. My master and mistress would tell me about dogs that they had owned and my mistress showed me some pictures. Tears would come into her eyes, so I know they must have been good dogs.

When spring came, robins and blue birds came also, and I could hear the "Bob White" calling close by, but my master told me not to hunt them, because they were raising families and must not be disturbed.

That summer my master and mistress had planted a fine garden. The robins were living high on the strawberries and I wanted to drive them away, but my mistress said, "No, Dave, let them alone; their songs will more than pay for all they eat."

One day while my master and I were sitting on the porch, some young quail came out of a nearby field on to the lawn. I had caught the scent before I had seen them, and came to a point, but the master said, "No, Dave, we will wait until they grow big." That was the day when my master and mistress entertained the children. She shot for them and then I would do all my stunts. I always loved little children and did my best to please them. My master told them stories, then refreshments were served and they all wanted to divide with me. I got more than my share.

South For Winter.

My mistress told me one day we were going South for the winter. I was put in a new crate, had plenty of fresh straw for a bed and a can of fresh water to drink. That was one thing my master and mistress would see to—that their dogs always had plenty of fresh water. No one but a dog who has had to go without water can appreciate what that means. I was locked in my crate and then put on a train. My master told me we were going to Florida. Of course, I didn't know how far that was and felt very much worried, as it was my first trip in a crate, but felt better when my master came into the baggage car some time during the night. He brought me a nice bone which he said my mistress sent me. Next morning my mistress came in to see me and as we had to stop a short time, she took me out on the leash and gave me a nice run and more fresh water.

When we arrived in Florida, a day later, I found it very hot and also found that a dog had some things to annoy him that were not very pleasant—fleas, ticks and red bugs were plentiful. We had a very bad hotel and we missed the comforts we were accustomed to. I had my own rug and slept in the bathroom. We hunted four days a week and had good sport, but my shoulder and right leg went back on me again, so that I could only go hunting about three days a week, and then I could only hunt about four hours.

One day I heard my master shoot, and went to see what he had fired at. I found he had killed a rattlesnake. He made me understand what it was and that I must never go close to one, and I never did. Another day I heard my mistress scream and shoot. I was working on some birds at the time, but ran back to see what had happened and found she had killed a big rattler. He had struck at her and she hadn't time to put the gun to her shoulder, so she fired from the hip and cut his head off. I had often seen her shoot that way when she was giving exhibitions. This snake measured seven feet, four inches. My master and mistress killed five others that season and we were all glad when the hunting season was over, and we longed to get back to our Maryland home.

I spent a quiet summer. There was nothing for me to do but bask in the sunshine when it was cold and lie under a shade tree when it was hot. When fall came I heard my master say we were going South. I was sorry to hear that, as I thought we were going back to Florida, and I was pleased to find out we were going to North Carolina instead. So trunks were packed, my crate was filled with straw and once more I was loaded into a baggage car and we started south, arriving at Pinehurst next day. After giving me a run, my master put me in a kennel. There was a name printed on the door of my room. I heard my master read it. He looked at me and said "That name is California Bell Boy, the First, he was your grandsire. At one time he was owned by the man who owns about all of Pinehurst now."

No More Kennel.

I knew I was going to like the place. Everyone was so nice to me. A few days later I met the manager of the hotel, and did a few stunts for him and his friends. Then he told my mistress I was too nice a dog to stay in a kennel, so my mistress put my rug in the bathroom, and for seven winters that was my home. I was the only dog allowed in the hotel, and I am sure I never abused that privilege. Although there were more than five hundred rooms, I could always find my own. I made a lot of friends. Everyone was so kind to me and now I look back and know that the most pleasant part of my life was spent at Pinehurst. My mistress gave several shooting exhibitions while we were there. She had taught me to hold an apple on my head while she shot it off. When she shot the apple I always managed to catch the biggest piece before it got to the ground. We always had a large audience and my stunts seemed to please them, and I know it pleased my master and mistress, so I felt well repaid for any risks run by me in holding the apple, which was little, if any, as I had full confidence in my mistress' marksmanship.

During my first two winters there I had many days in the field. Hunting was good and it was a nice country to hunt over, plenty of water, and no burrs or briars. On account of my lame shoulder I could only hunt a few hours and every second day, and my master and mistress decided not to hunt me any more. By that time I knew where there were several coveys, and so in the morning when I saw my master stealing out with his hunting coat and gun I would wait until he was started then I started to find some birds alone. I hunted and ran wild all day, stayed out until dark, then came limping home wet and tired. My mistress didn't whip me, just asked me wasn't I ashamed—and I was. Then she washed and combed me.

Next two days I was so sore and stiff I could hardly walk, and promised I would not go self-hunting again, but in less than a week I ran away again and continued to do so. I was always laid up for days after I had run away. I was never very far from home, as there were several coveys near town that were never hunted, so I had no trouble in finding them. My master and mistress scolded me, but never whipped me, although I know that I deserved to have been punished. I heard my master say, "It is the call of the wild, he can't help it."

But one day when I stayed out later than usual my mistress lost her patience and told me that if I ran away again she would surely whip me. I could tell by her looks that she meant it and it was some weeks before I ran away again.

Afraid To Go Home.

When I came back late I didn't go near the hotel. The manager had a cottage near-by, so I went there instead. I had done most of my hunting in the swamp that day and must have been a sorry-looking dog. I was not surprised when they wouldn't let me in, but I finally convinced them that I was not a tramp dog, so they opened the door far enough to let them see. Then I heard the lady say, "It's Dave. He has been hunting again and is afraid to go home." The manager went to the phone and I heard him say, "Dave is here. If you will promise not to whip him I will bring him home." They brought me back to the hotel. My master and mistress didn't scold me, but I know they felt hurt. I was sorry and promised myself I wouldn't run away again, and it was a long time before I did do so.

Summer came again. We all went to New Hampshire. I had heard a lot of talk about war, but couldn't understand what it all meant. My master and mistress tried to tell me, but I could not then or now understand why one half of the world should try to kill the other half. Every day soldiers with guns were marching and training, while cannons roared and shook the earth. I heard my master and mistress talking it over. My mistress said, "Dave, we will have to work for Uncle Sam. I know you are an English setter, but you are an American dog. You will have to do your share." So for two summers my mistress worked for the Red Cross and earned a lot of money for them. People would let me get the scent of a bill and then hide it. If I found it, it went to the Red Cross. I never missed finding and was told that I earned $1,629 that way.

While working in the cantonments I always slept with my mistress in the Y. W. C. A. building, while the master slept in the Y. M. C. A. We were treated fine while there, but I never knew there were so many guns and soldiers.

Proud of His Job.

I was a proud dog when I was allowed to do my bit. My master received some nice letters from the war officials and commanders of the different cantonments in which I had received honorable mention. At the finish of our engagement we again started for North Carolina. We were glad to get back there. My master had bought a new hunting dog named Fred. He had been running in field trials and was very fast. We soon became very good friends and I liked him very much, as he was a high-class, well-bred and well-behaved dog. I was sorry when my master sold him, but I understood he was too fast for that country.

I suppose dogs and people run very much alike. I know during my travels I have met all kinds of dogs—good, bad and very bad. My master tells me, however, that humans are the same. They also told me I could save a lot of trouble by minding my own business, which I tried to do, but many times when I had little curs running and snapping at my feet I found it very hard to live up to it. But I knew it would not be to my credit to whip some poor little mutt because he had no brains.

There was one kind of a dog my master always cautioned me not to trust. That was the so-called police dog—really the German shepherd dog, whose owners found were worth more money by changing their name and nationality. They are part wolf, cowardly and treacherous, always ready to jump on a small dog and bite the hand that feeds them. There was one down where I was one winter and I had often seen him, but as I always kept my eye on him he let me alone. It seems that he made friends with a part airedale mutt. They had chewed up several small dogs and killed one. Neither my master or I had heard of this. One morning when I was having my walk they both jumped on me. Either one of them was much larger than I was. By the time my master caught up I was badly chewed, but I had the satisfaction of chasing the police dog into his own house. My mistress spent several weeks doctoring my wounds. A short time after, the German dog bit his mistress and was sent away.

Summer again; so we left for the North. We all spent several months on a Long Island horse ranch. The owner, his wife and three daughters were delightful people. There were several horses on the ranch. I spent hours there every day and had lots of fun pointing pigeons. Everyone was so kind to all of us, and we knew we were welcome, and I often dream about them and wonder if we ever will meet again. If not, dear Dorothy, sweet Paula and dainty Carie will always hold a place in my memory.

As my master and mistress had some business in New York City, we spent a few months there. To me it seemed years. I for one don't envy any dog that lives there. Every one I met there was either wearing a muzzle or on a leash. We were fortunate in living on the Riverside Drive. I soon made friends with the policemen there and they were very nice to me, and I had some few privileges that the other dogs did not have, but I was glad when we left New York. I can readily understand why dogs go mad there.

Working at Maps.

Evenings I could see my master and mistress working over maps, making plans for the winter. When I found we were not going back to North Carolina I was sorry, but my master told me my mistress needed a change of climate, and we were again going to Florida. I was sorry to hear this, as I had not forgotten my other trip there, and was not very keen on going back, but of course it was to help my mistress and I was satisfied. Lad joined me in Philadelphia and we all started by boat to Florida. As our crates were together, my master came and took us on deck every day. We had a very nice trip to Jacksonville. There I was put on a train, while my master and mistress went on in an automobile. My master told us he would see us that night, and I was disappointed when I didn't see him that night or the next.

Two days later my master came and we were glad to see him. He looked tired and was very sad. He patted us both and told me my mistress had been hurt badly in an automobile accident and that she was in a hospital a hundred miles from where we were. Next day my master and I left for the hospital, but we couldn't take Lad along. There was no place to keep him. We were sorry to leave him, and my master told him he would come after him, which he did seven weeks later.

It was late at night when we got to the hospital, but I wanted to see my mistress and I was sure she wanted to see me. My, but we were glad to see each other. But she looked very feeble and could only put out one hand to stroke my head. By putting my feet on a chair I managed to get close enough to lick her ear. My master and I had a nice clean room across from the hospital. He told me all about the accident. I was allowed to go into the hospital every day and spent several hours with my mistress. I didn't like the nurses there, as they seemed rough and hurt my mistress when they moved her. We spent several [weeks] there before my mistress could sit up again.

My mistress could now move around by using crutches and she brushed and combed me every day. She was always so gentle and careful in combing and brushing me that I enjoyed having it done. I often wondered if any other dog had a mistress so good and gentle as mine.

The hunting season is now ended and Lad has been sent north to his Meadowbrook home. I went with my master to see him off and I miss him very much. I could always tell when it was Saturday, because it is my bath day, and I know today is Sunday, as I can hear the church bells ringing. My mistress has given me a brushing and combing. It is a grand day and as my master is waiting for me, I am anxious to get out.

To the Happy Hunting Grounds.

With a master and mistress such as I had my life was a pleasure until—

————

There ended Dave's story. His career was ended in an automobile accident at Leesburg, Fla. His resting place is a grave in a dog cemetery marked by a stone bearing the simple name—Dave.

What's Missing From the Article

While the version of *The Life of Dave* published in the *Newark Sunday Call* on June 24, 1923 captures the heart of Dave's story, the original booklet includes several passages that did not appear in the newspaper article. Most differences are minor—variations in grammar, punctuation, or word choice (e.g., bath room vs. bathroom, twelve mile vs. twelve-miles', have vs. undergo an operation)—and are not expanded upon here.

The section titles below were created by the editor to reflect the themes of each excerpt. Quoted passages from the booklet appear indented, while editorial commentary is presented in standard format.

Dave Gets Lost

Dave's loyalty and instinct were shaped by early moments of confusion and longing. One such story, absent from the newspaper article, appears in the booklet and reveals how easily a devoted dog could be misled by hope.

> It was then that I met with a mishap that came near losing my new home. Birds were scarce and I was getting away ahead of Frank hunting by myself, in a piece of woods, when I saw what I thought was my master's hunting wagon, going along the road. The horse was the same color and there was a woman and a man in the wagon. I felt sure it was my master and mistress, and I ran for miles behind, hoping they would take me in. But when they turned into a house and got out, I found it wasn't them, and I was a very tired and broken-hearted dog, for I didn't want to lose the first real friends I ever had.

> My old master told me, when I was puppy, that if I ever got lost to go back to the place where I last saw him; so I made my way best I could to the place where we had lunch. It was after dark when I got to the place. After resting a short time I tried to get my bearing and started to find the town where I had slept the night before and that I had seen only once. It was dark and raining very hard. I got off the road twice, but found my mistake before going far. After several hours of

hard traveling I saw lights and knew I was coming to a town, and was glad to find it was the right one. It took me some time to locate the stable. I finally found it and was thinking of the warm straw bed, but when I tried to get in the door was shut. Frank heard me and barked which cheered me up some. I was cold, wet and hungry. I finally found a wagon in an open shed and got in the wagon, where my master found me in the morning when he brought Frank his breakfast.

I was glad to see him and I know he was glad to see me. He brought me to see my mistress in the room at the hotel. She rubbed me dry with towels while my master got some breakfast. Then she combed the briars out of my hair and rubbed something on my feet, as they were very sore. I heard her say that I had fleas, so my master got something that didn't smell very good and put it in a tub of warm water. This would kill the insects that might be on me. Then my mistress gave me the first real bath I ever had, after which she wrapped me up in a blanket and I slept for hours without scratching, something I had never done before.

Then my master took me out for a walk, but we had only gone a short distance when I saw Chick coming out of a house. He saw me at the same time. My, it seemed good to see him again. He joined us and we had a fine time. He told me he had a nice home and a good master. When he found out where I was living he came to see me several times every day, for he, like myself, made few friends among dogs and we found it hard to keep from fighting with some of the town mongrels. We were bird dogs, not fighters, but when we had a fight we stuck together and they soon learned to let us alone. Chick and I had many hunting days together and were staunch friends for years. While hunting with my master he spent many hours teaching me what I should and what I shouldn't do, and I tried to understand his every wish. When I made mistakes he didn't whip me, but tried to show me my mistakes. When I did what he wished me to do he always showed he was pleased by calling me in, patting my head and stroking my ears.

A Maryland Summer

The booklet includes a paragraph describing a summer in Maryland. While not dramatic, it adds environmental texture to Dave's journey—reminding us that his travels weren't just emotional, but physical and seasonal.

Summer found me still at the Maryland home. The weather was very hot, but there was a very nice river in front of the house and a nice sandy beach, where I could swim to my heart's content. Chick continued to come to see me and my master would throw sticks into the water for us to retrieve. I had located a few coveys of quail and was wondering how long it would be before my master would take his gun and let me show him where to find them. But I never had a chance to do so.

The Pointer Puppy

In the booklet, there's a paragraph about another dog—a pointer puppy owned by Dave's masters. The puppy's energy and speed left Dave struggling to keep up, a contrast that adds nuance to his role in the household.

Later my master showed me a pointer puppy that was given him. He was very small and timid, so I was nice to him and let him play with me. Now he is a fine strong fellow and a very good bird dog. We traveled together many miles and I spent two weeks with him at Meadowbrook Kennels while my master and mistress were away on a business trip. I have hunted with him but he is young and strong, while I am getting along in years, so I can't keep up with him. My master and mistress say I am a better retriever than he is, as I find the dead birds, which gives me a good day's sport.

Fleas and Mange in Florida

The booklet includes several references to fleas and mange affecting both Dave and Lad during their time in Florida. These aren't glamorous details, but they're honest—and they reflect the toll of climate and hardship on even the most resilient animals.

About twice a week I was dipped in something that didn't smell very nice. It must have been good, for it kept the fleas off.

Someone opened our crates and let us out, but the place was very dirty and we were soon covered with fleas.

...only to find him (Lad) eaten up with fleas and mange.

We all moved over to the place Lad was when my mistress was able to sit up. My, but he was glad to see us. My master worked on him for a week before he got cured of the mange. Then when he was washed he was all right and we could go out and play together. He went hunting many times with my master. I didn't go on an all-day hunt, as the weather was very hot and I couldn't stand it, but my master did take me out evenings near the town, where I could find a few birds without working too hard.

...but no dog can keep free of fleas in Florida. No matter how hard my mistress tried they would get into my hair.

In the Newspapers: Dave and Annie in Florida

Newspaper articles of Dave's passing and Annie Oakley's time in Florida and Leesburg

Printed from "The Tampa Tribune" March 4, 1923, page TWO-B

"Dave" Annie Oakley's little dog, known the country over as the Red Cross dog, that brought in thousands of dollars for the Red Cross during the war, lost his life in an automobile accident Sunday evening. Miss Oakley and her husband, Frank Butler, have been stopping at the Lake View ever since she was discharged from the hospital at Daytona following an automobile accident several months ago, from which she received injuries that still cause her much suffering.

"Dave" was not only his mistress' pet and companion but was so famous that his name starred in the headlines of all the big dailies a few years ago and oftimes his photo adorned the front pages. He was scarce less known that his famous mistress who is the champion woman rifle shot of the world and withal a sweet little woman.

"Dave" met the fate of many human beings; he got in front of a rapidly moving automobile Sunday night and was killed. Having no children Mr. and Mrs. Butler had made of "Dave" a pet , a hero, a pal, an in his death they feel the sorrow that parents would feel for the loss of a child. All during the world war he had been the constant companion and helper of his mistress in raising funds for the Red Cross and war work and people would often give because of the little fellow that would have contributed for no other reason.

With the same tender consideration that parents show for a child the body of the unfortunate little fellow was prepared for burial; his remains were taken to a spot in George Winter's beautiful orange grove and there interred. Mr. and Mrs. Butler will rear a neat little monument over the grave of their pet telling those who might pass this way that here lies the body of one of man's faithful friends an one who did his bit to give true democracy to the world.

Printed from "The Miami Daily Metropolis" March 28, 1923, page ELEVEN

DAVE, WONDER DOG HIT BY AUTOMOBILE, DIES

During the War Dog Owned By Famous Annie Oakley Did Great Red Cross Service

---

When a dog gets in the path of a fast moving automobile, the canine comes to an untimely finish and not more than once in a million times will you find anything about the death of the dog in the daily press. The one time occurred recently at Leesburg, Fla., when "Dave" the setter, trained and owned by Annie Oakley, one of the greatest shots the world has ever known, was struck by an automobile. "Dave" during the war became famous as the Red Cross dog. His stunts brought in many thousands of dollars for the Red Cross. The things he did caused headlines in the leading newspapers, and when "Dave" was bumped by an automobile these things were all remembered by writers. And just to show what is thought of "Dave" a monument has been erected over his grave in Leesburg. Miss Oakley was once handed a blank check and told to insert her own figures for "Dave." She tore up the check. There wasn't enough money in the world to purchase the dog, she said.

Printed from the "St. Petersburg Times" November 11, 1922, page TWELVE

ANNIE OAKLEY HURT

DAYTONA, Nov. 10.—Annie Oakley, of Leesburg, Fla., former horse woman with Buffalo Bill's Wild West shows, is in a serious condition at a local hospital suffering from a broken hip received when an automobile overturned on the Dixie Highway north of Daytona, yesterday.

Printed from the "Newark Sunday Call" November 26, 1922, page 29

Annie Oakley Injured In Florida Auto Crash

———

Annie Oakley, famous woman rifle shot, who formerly resided in Nutley, is still in a private hospital at Daytona, Fla., suffering from a fractured hip as the result of an automobile accident on the Dixie Highway, near the Florida resort, on November 9.

Miss Oakley, together with Frank E. Butler, her husband, and Mr. and Mrs. J. J. Storer and a Mr. Young, were on their way to Leesburgh*, where the members of the party intended to spend the winter. After passing an automobile at a point forty-six miles north of Daytona, Mr. Young, who was piloting a big Cadillac, attempted to turn back on a brick road and losing control of the car, it jumped over an embankment and turned turtle. Miss Oakley was pinned underneath the upturned car but none of the other occupants was injured.

B. Benson of Fort Pierce was following closely behind, and after assisting in extricating Miss Oakley from the wreck took her to Daytona, where Dr. Bohannon set the fractured hip. It is said that she will be compelled to remain in the hospital from four to six weeks.

** The original article spells the town as "Leesburgh." The correct spelling is Leesburg.*

Printed from "The Tampa Tribune" February 25, 1923, page FIVE-B. This article was printed on the day Dave was killed.

ANNIE OAKLEY GOOD SHOT NOW AS EVER

———

VISITS LEESBURG FOR RECUPERATING

———

World Famous Rifle Shot, Mrs. Frank Butler, Escapes Death Four Times

LEESBURG, Fla., Feb. 24.—"I can shoot just as good as I ever could. I have been near death at four different times because of accidents, but somehow the Lord manages to pull me through."

So says Mrs. Frank Butler when a visitor sits down to chat with her at her bedside in Lake View hotel.

Mrs. Butler? She is none other than Annie Oakley, known the world over as a celebrated rifle shot and who has won more medals with her rifles than any commander ever won with sword and daring on the battlefield.

Annie Oakley has been in Leesburg for the last three months, the victim of an automobile accident. She was injured on the way from Jacksonville to Leesburg. Her hip was broken, and as soon as she was able to be out of the hospital at Daytona she was brought here.

"You know that I was near death four times," she asks of the new visitor. "My, yes! Each time it was the result of an accident. The dear Lord always has pulled me through, though."

And then she told how her hair became white as snow in the short space of one night.

Hair Turns White

"I was on a train in Virginia. It was wrecked and I was nearly killed. In one night my hair turned as white as the driven snow. The accident happened at about 2 o'clock in the morning, and at 5 o'clock that afternoon my hair was entirely white.

"That was the worst accident I ever was in, but I had three other ones. Still I can shoot just as good as ever I could. My eyes don't bother me a bit. Why, just before my recent accident—that is, last fall—I gave exhibitions of five minutes' duration—five of them—at Brockton Fair, near Boston. During those five performances 98,000 persons saw me shoot. For those twenty-five minutes I received $700, but I have done much better than that before."

Annie Oakley is in her late fifties, but even her white hair cannot make the stranger believe she is more than forty. She was born near Greenville, O., in 1866*, and as a little girl learned to shoot in the woods surrounding her home. She declared she always had a keen eye and a steady nerve. When she was sixteen years old she married Frank E. Butler, and it was he who induced her to enter the lists as a professional shooter. She soon won country-wide plaudits. Following a year's tour she joined the Wild West Show conducted by Buffalo Bill, continuing with that aggregation for seventeen years. In that time she demonstrated many times that she was the champion woman shot of the world.

Modern scholarship places Annie Oakley's birth year as 1860. The article reproduced here contains the original (incorrect) date.

Printed from "The Evening Bulletin" (Philadelphia) March 13, 1923, page 30. Just a few weeks after Dave was killed, Annie Oakley appeared before a Philadelphia Phillies spring training game at Leesburg's Cooke Field. The Phillies trained there from 1922 to 1924, and this exhibition took place during their second season in town. The following article captures Oakley's remarkable return to performing in early 1923.

The Evening Bulletin

Annie Oakley, Sixty and Crippled, Astonishes Phils with Marksmanship

LEESBURG, Fla., March 13—For sheer pluck and determination to carry on in the face of almost insurmountable physical difficulties, Annie Oakley stands virtually supreme among women who have long been in the public eye.

White haired, nearly sixty years of age, forced to walk on crutches and with her face drawn from long suffering, Annie Oakley today declares she intends to be her former self again.

"As soon as I get well enough, and I am going to get well, I intend to keep up the work I have been doing for the past seven years—that of giving exhibitions for charity."

With her broken hip only recently knitted, the tendons of her right leg and foot pulled out of place, Annie Oakley, undaunted, clear-eyed with head erect was assisted from her automobile by her husband, Frank E. Butler, just inside Cooke Field, the training grounds of the Phillies.

"I haven't shot since October 8," she said as she slowly made her way on crutches to the stand where her rifles and shot guns were. "Still I think my eye is good and maybe I'll be able to shoot fairly straight."

The exhibition which followed would have been wonderful under any circumstances but considering she abandoned her crutches and put virtually all of her weight on her left leg, made her performance little short of miraculous.

———

> Her first stunt was to hit pennies tossed in the air at a distance
> of twenty feet. She did not miss twenty-five of the little discs.

———

When she hit them, they went spinning across the diamond, where a riot ensued among the little colored* boys who engaged in a mad scramble for the one-cent pieces.

At a further distance she shot metal discs about the size of a silver dollar, hitting them on the top, bottom or side edges, as the spectators would request.

She finished by throwing five eggs in the air with her left hand and then breaking them before hitting the ground. This stunt she performed several times while the Philly players applauded.

She has never seen the Drexel Institute girls of Philadelphia shoot, but says she has often seen pictures of them.

———

> "I only wish I had the opportunity to give them a little instruc-
> tion," she says. "I can tell by the photographs I have seen they
> do not hold their rifles quite right. I could rectify that easily
> and make them better than they are, even if they have never
> been beaten."

———

Annie Oakley began shooting when at the age of eleven, she did all the family hunting and trapping for the family, which lived in Northern Ohio.

At sixteen, she was married to Frank E. Butler. "I didn't teach her to shoot," he says, "because she could have taught me even then, although I was supposed to be a crack shot myself in those days. I simply got her a position and she did the rest."

Annie Oakley's nerve has been shown hundreds of times, but never more prominently than on one occasion when she was with the Buffalo Bill Wild West Show. Her right collarbone was broken in an accident, but rather than disappoint the crowd, she turned around and shot left-handed, doing all of her stunts perfectly.

* *This term appears in the original article. It is reproduced verbatim to preserve the historical record, though it is recognized today as outdated and offensive.*

Once after an exhibition in Berlin she met former Kaiser Wil-helm, who was then Crown Prince of Germany. At his sugges-tion, she shot the ashes from his cigarette which he held in his mouth at a distance of thirty paces.

ANNIE OAKLEY AS SHE LOOKS TODAY

Champion markswoman of world visits Phillies' training camp at Lees-burg, Fla., and proves her eye as unerr-ing as ever.

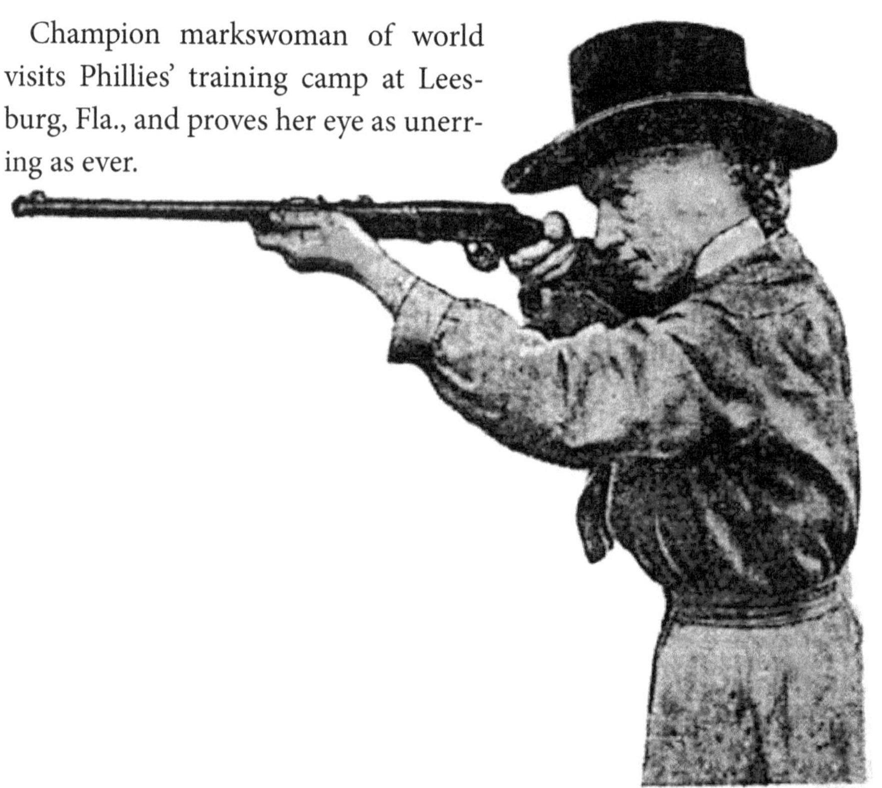

Ban Johnson First Called Free Pass an "Annie Oakley"

One time in New York Ban Johnson was standing at the pass gate when a man presented a "non-transferable" ticket. Every time it was used the ticket taker punched a hole in it.

There were so many holes in this one Ban Johnson remarked: "Well, that looks more like a target than a base ball pass."

Now all free tickets are "Annie Oakleys."

Printed from the "Newark Sunday Call" February 25, 1912, page 48. The dog pictured is not Dave.

ANNIE OAKLEY'S HUNTING DOG
POINTING A LARGE RATTLESNAKE

Annie Oakley (Mrs. Frank Butler), formerly a resident of Nutley, had a remarkable experience a few weeks ago while hunting birds. Mr. and Mrs. Butler have been in the South for a number of weeks, taking advantage of the "on" season to enjoy some good hunting. This is the way Annie Oakley keeps herself in trim for her wonderful achievements as an expert shot during the season that she is on the road with Buffalo Bill's Wild West or some other troupe of entertainers. One day not long ago when she was ranging the fields with her dog, looking for game, the dog suddenly took the point and became rigid. It was some time before it was discovered that he was pointing at a rattlesnake, and a huge one. One of the men in the party saw the snake first and shot it. The picture shows the dog pointing the reptile. It was about six feet long, and Mrs. Butler now has its skin.

Annie Oakley will come north to New York in time to take part in the Sportsmen's Show, which begins on March 1.

Printed from the "Newark Sunday Call" March 7, 1915, page 49

Annie Oakley's Story of Winter Hunting in Florida

Annie Oakley and the Skin of
· the Big Rattlesnake ·

Hunting in Florida has been the winter sport this year of Annie Oakley, who is Mrs. Frank E. Butler in private life. Writing recently to a friend in this city from the Graystone, at Kissimmee, on Lake Tohopekaliga, she says she and Mr. Butler have lived and hunted in that section a greater portion of the winter for the last four years and its charms never grow less for them. Annie Oakley is known the world over as an expert with rifle and shotgun, having given public exhibitions during a long period of years with the biggest shows under canvas in all parts of the United States and Europe. When in this section of the country her home for many years has been in Nutley, and she and her husband have many friends in and around Newark. Some of them have recently asked the couple by letter for information about the shooting in the part of Florida which they visit, and the description given herewith of some of their experiences and of their views was sent to the Sunday Call in order that it may reach all those who desire to know and who are interested in anything that Annie Oakley takes up.

"My husband and myself have hunted over fourteen countries on all kinds of game," is the opening sentence in a letter sent for publication, "but I know of no one State or place where a sportsman can find a greater variety of game than can be found in Florida.

"While quail shooting is the principal sport hereabouts, there are also snipe, doves, wild turkeys, deer, bear, wildcat, 'possum, fox and so many rabbits that scarcely anyone cares to bother shooting them. With the exception of the wild turkeys, all the game here is smaller than the same species found in the Northern States. The Florida deer generally weighs about 150 pounds, never more than two hundred, at maturity. It is un-usually pretty and resembles the German roebuck.

"In quail shooting the bag limit is twenty birds each day for each per-son, and we have seldom failed to return to the hotel with that number. In fact, for the last four years we have furnished free quail to the guests at the hotels in which we have stopped, and they have appreciated them greatly. Our splendid record in the fields and woods is in a large mea-sure due to the great work of my brace of dogs. They are named Fred Stone and Dave Montgomery and are shown in the photograph which I inclose, which was taken while they were ranging over one of our favor-ite hunting grounds.

"We vary our sport quite frequently, and the other day we returned with a magnificent specimen of wild turkey, which was killed by Mr. Butler. It weighed eighteen pounds and was in fine condition, and made an unusually good dinner. We also got a full-grown deer recently, a fine specimen and plump and rather above the average condition for food purposes. The hunt which resulted in getting him was a delightful one, too. A bit of spice is often given to the hunting by getting a 'possum or going after snipe or other kinds of game. That is one of the beauties of the hunting down here—one is not confined continually to seeking and getting one kind of game, and when a wildcat hunt is on there is, of course, always a chance for some excitement out of the ordinary. An occasional fox hunt, too, adds spirit to the life, especially if the chase is a good one and the quarry is a veteran and quite up to all the tricks of evading the dogs and their followers.

"But, while Florida has an ideal winter climate and the hunting is all that the most expert or enthusiastic could wish for, it must be remembered that there are some drawbacks to the situation, and one must not think that there are no dangers in tracking the woods and the fields in search of game. One of them is the prevalence of Florida rattlesnakes and the moccasin cotton-mouth snake, which is equally dangerous and poisonous with the rattler. To be struck by either of these varieties is sure death. The diamond-back rattler is more plentiful, and therefore more to be feared than the moccasin.

"Three years ago while we were down here I had one of the best dogs I ever owned—and that is saying a great deal, for I have owned and hunted over some of the greatest dogs that ever ranged the brush in this or any other country—struck by a cotton-mouth snake and killed. Since then I have been more careful than ever when hunting or strolling through the woods or fields, but in spite of my caution I came nearer to stepping on a rattler a few weeks ago than I care to again.

"Contrary to the general impression as to the habits of the rattler, this one gave me absolutely no warning of its presence or its intention to strike. I happened to look at the ground less than a pace distant and saw the rattler. It was coiled and ready to strike. Another step forward and I would have received the stroke. I never did such quick thinking in my life as was crowded into that second. I sprang backward and at the same instant raised my gun and fired quickly.

"The shot went true, and the rattler was killed where it lay, its head being blown off. I took it back to the hotel with me and had it skinned, and the skin tacked on a board. Without the head it measured exactly seven feet and four inches in length. I am sending you a photograph of the mounted skin. Not until I had finished my hunting for the day did it dawn upon me that I had had a really narrow escape from certain death. Why the rattler gave no warning sound when I approached, and it had made ready to strike, I have found no one who can explain. The slightest false move on my part, or failure of my quick shot, would have resulted disastrously for me.

"Another matter that I want to call to the attention of my personal friends in the North, and to others who may read my letter, is that the curse of Florida is the land sharks who operate chiefly in the Northern States and through the West. They print alluring advertisements in pamphlet form, and they catch the gullible by the thousands. We have met hundreds of persons here who were making their way back to their homes in the North after having been induced to come down here by the false statements made to them. In many cases their trip South meant the investment and spending of every dollar they had in the world.

"Of course, they did not see what they were buying until they got here, and then they found that the land for which they had paid was either under water or so poor that nothing would grow on it. Uncle Sam and his Federal government machinery has recently put a few of the Florida land swindling fraternity in jail."

Leesburg Monuments

After Dave was killed, Annie Oakley tried to have her beloved companion buried at Lone Oak Cemetery, but the request was denied. Instead, she laid him to rest on the property of friends, Mr. and Mrs. George Winter, a few miles away, marking the spot with a simple stone bearing his name. That original marker has since been moved to Lone Oak Cemetery, fulfilling Annie's original wish, and a monument now stands over it telling his story.

The monument says:

Dave "Butler"

Annie Oakley's and Frank Butler's Beloved English Setter
Died Feb. 25, 1923
From a car accident in Leesburg, FL

Annie wanted Dave to be buried at Lone Oak Cemetery
but the officials said no.
Annie buried her dog a few miles away. In 2021 Dave's
stone was recovered and placed here at Lone Oak Cemetery,
where Annie Oakley desired.

In 1917, Dave toured WWI U.S. training areas with
Annie, "doing his bit for his country and bringing sunshine to
the hearts of thousands of our dear boys."

"He awaits us both in the Happy Hunting Ground. His
memory is one of the sweetest we have ever known."

Annie died in 1926 and Frank 3 weeks later.

VISITING THE MONUMENT:
The monument and stone are located within the Pet Haven Memorial Gardens section of Lone Oak Cemetery, 306 Thomas Avenue, Leesburg, FL 34748. The cemetery is gated and open only during posted daytime hours, so visitors should call ahead or confirm current hours before arriving. Lone Oak Cemetery is a peaceful and beautifully maintained memorial cemetery, and the visit is meaningful in its own right.

While Leesburg may have been only a small chapter in the remarkable life of Annie Oakley, she remains a meaningful part of the city's history. Every few years, local and regional newspapers revisit her time in Florida—especially her winters in Leesburg—and Dave's tragic death on that February morning is always remembered. To honor her connection to the community, a bronze sculpture of Annie Oakley and Dave stands behind the Leesburg Public Library.

The sculpture was commissioned by the Friends of the Leesburg Library and funded through donations from community members and the Friends' considerable fundraising efforts.

The Leesburg Chamber of Commerce, Leesburg Partnership, and the Leesburg Center for the Arts assisted with the fundraising effort.

The cost for the Annie Oakley and Dave sculpture was $60,000, which represented a reduced price that allowed the artist to reproduce the work and sell it elsewhere.

Though the sculpture was created and installed during the construction of the new city library, no city public funds were used to pay for the sculpture.

VISITING THE MONUMENT:

The sculpture is located at the Leesburg Public Library, 100 East Main Street, Leesburg, FL 34748, on the north side of the building and accessible without entering the library. The parking lot and parking garage immediately to the west occupy the former site of the Lake View Hotel, where Annie, Frank, and Dave stayed during their time in Leesburg.

References & Image Credits

References:

The Life of Dave. 5th printing, 2021.
Originally reprinted by The Garst Museum, The Darke County Historical Society, Inc., Greenville, Ohio.
Printed by Commercial Printing Company, Greenville, Ohio.

All newspaper articles reproduced in this book are cited immediately before each article.

The editor consulted the following sources to obtain the original newspaper material:

- The *Newark Sunday Call*
  Newark History Archives — https://newark.historyarchives.online/

- Florida Newspapers
  University of Florida Digital Collections — https://newspapers.uflib.ufl.edu/

- *The Evening Bulletin* (Philadelphia, PA)
  Free Library of Philadelphia - www.freelibrary.org/

Image Credits:

Images appearing within the reproduced articles originate from the referenced newspaper sources.

- Front cover, page 4 (top)
  Heritage Auctions — historical.ha.com

- Back cover, page 4 (bottom)
  Courtesy photo/screenshot from Friends of the Leesburg Public Library video

- Pages 34, 36, and 37
  Photographs taken August 22, 2025 by the editor

Acknowledgements

The editor gratefully acknowledges the many individuals and institutions whose assistance made this book possible.

Special thanks to the Leesburg Public Library, especially Dusty Matthews, Director, and Rachel Costantino, Adult Services Supervisor, for their guidance and support throughout the research process.

Appreciation is also extended to the Leesburg Heritage Society and Historical Museum, Lone Oak Cemetery, and the Newspapers and Microfilm Division of the Free Library of Philadelphia for access to archival materials and historical records.

Sincere thanks to Andi Purvis, City Clerk of the City of Leesburg, for her help in locating municipal information related to this project.

Finally, the editor wishes to recognize the many others—both in Leesburg and beyond—who contributed in ways large and small to bringing this book to completion and helping preserve the scattered history surrounding Dave's tragic passing and the time Annie (Oakley) Butler, her husband Frank, and their beloved dogs spent in Florida.